Vetted Love

A Poetic Anthology

I. Stevens

DEDICATION

This collection of poetry is dedicated to all of the people in my life with whom I have been blessed to share this multifaceted and mystic precept of love.

CONTENTS

FOREWORD

"Love sought is good, but giv'n unsought is better."
~ William Shakespeare, *Twelfth Night*

Vetted love has restorative and mystic properties of celestial worth and issue. Time spent in vetted love is never wasted, and over the spectrum of time itself, vetted love slowly develops.

Vetted love is tried, true, and its roots run deep into our souls. It is substantive and holds up to inquiry and scrutiny.

It weathers the storms of human frailty, expands in the togetherness of fellowship, and endures through lonely nights and the distant separation of miles.

Vetted love is both seen and felt in ways that move our emotions and touch our hearts beyond that of mere romantic gestures. It is best seen and reserved for those people who are most precious to our human connections and our spiritual fulfillment. However, it can find its resting place in music, literature, places, sports, recreation, and countless other aspects of our human experience and existence.

We often feel vetted love for our families, friends of old, churches, synagogues and houses of our worship, schools and universities of our attendance. It exists in professions of a lifetime, branches of dutiful service paid, and a country where homage in birth was made, heritage embraced, and even sacrifice given.

The strength of vetted love requires absorbent qualities of endurance and unconditional acceptance of human decisions made. It is often tested with questions of how and why, but never diminished in value with the responsive abundance of understanding and acceptance. For vetted love requires of us an exact proportion of choice in what was first lovingly gifted to us . . . the heavenly light of God's grace.

I. Stevens

Vetted Love

Yes, it is tonight life claims her glory, for yesterday is the dust of prior choice.

Self dissolved within the mist of dreams deferred and sadness too often found,

Yet hidden away in the shadows of minds and corners of bruised hearts,

The pulse of promise beats low, waiting to recapture a heavenly light. Shared acceptance of our flawed self is now absorbed beyond virtuous worth,

Seeking and once seen in a vision of conformed unity by penned verse. An emptiness perceived and stolen in time, as a nation's once fervor of proclaimed faith lies dormant.

Trusting now, the need of relationship must be the pushed premise of resolve.

For the stardust in our blood mixes with His sacrifice for our union of design,

Issue vetted love, strengthened through the bonds of our joint hope and purpose,

Then the tears of both justice and joy will blend togetherness among us all.

Forgiving struggles of weakness, mercy reigns and freedom of spirit sings again.

Brotherhood of Man

The miraculous works of God are seen first in the mere actions of men, as we challenge our hearts to seek more.

This is our new proclamation of faith to no longer lean on the certainty of dogmas past, but rely now on relational trust.

Challenging what we once found comfort in clinging to for solace, for today requires our forward steps of unison.

Brotherhood of man is our heavenly calling, for him we have seen and known, as ourselves, with weakness abound.

So choose faith, hope, and love not in words alone, but instead allow these to shine forth from within for charity to all.

For this is required of our professed love of humanity if a freedom's shore indeed awaits our dawning.

My Love Left the Moon

My love left the moon tonight and settled in the dark and void,
Dusting the heavens with memories of you and a wish unfulfilled.
Dreams of what were never meant to be, revisited with a smile,
Yet holding back a tear and daring once again to envision our lost love.

What is there in a night such as this, where the cool breeze longs to kiss the stars,
As I once longed to kiss your soften cheek, caressing more than mere beauty could bestow?
Time and space, as endless as the love we pledged, seeking only the mystic moment,
But feeling eternity was not enough for something so special as this precious now.

If only the knowledge of today could so easily be pressed against the window of time,
Perhaps then we could again dance the night in laughter and ease.
Watching the evening sky paint forever its masterpiece of awe and wonder,
Feeling hence, the purpose of our sharing will lean itself to hope for the dawning light of tomorrow.

Passing Tides

For a love gone by, which stole away in hidden hearts of a cold night, as tears now flow and hurt lies in false forbidden places where promise once thrived.

It is no longer reality to preserve what was declared before the intent of mankind, as angels sang and humanity proclaimed for the telling of all to believe.

Stated sadness of stained desire does not suffice to lay in restitution of deferred passions no longer shared, while visions of deceit haunt broken dreams.

Yet suns will rise and fall, as winter's impermanence is but a season away; for celestial comfort of light does not dismiss the position of adoring truth.

For just as the pace of passing tides are linked to the fullness of the moon, so too is the veracity of heavenly love and only makes its finding more worthy of delay.

The Light From Stars

The light from stars, kissed with celestial grace, fell down upon the common and creation cultivated anew.

Flowers grew in beauty bold, honey sweetened, and butterflies deepened in hue, with but the mention of her name.

The union of faith and family flourished with a child's touch, and her laughter launched dreams of regained hope.

With her smiles, we wept with joy, and with her tears we ran to her rescue, determined to cushion her life with love.

Through her eyes, we envisioned a brighter tomorrow, for a once darkened world that she will, no doubt, in betterment change.

And wrapped in her heart came the answers to all questions of truth and purpose that the heavens have whispered forever.

For my precious granddaughter, Stella.

The Old Barn

Lost and forever out of place, the old barn still stands weathered and
fading.
Its purpose now a forgotten truth, once served as a storing for brighter
days and dreams yet fulfilled.
The glory of its origin no longer seen, hidden by unforgiving time and
unwanted years.
Golden sun and aging winds have taken its boards and its beauty away
long ago,
And so its lingering toil and duty issued becomes a faint whisper onto
the newness of another generation.

Yet somewhere among its ruin, for those who care enough to envision,
a worthiness rests.
A strength that surpasses the weakness of humanity, a faith that we,
too, can endure still abounds.
For its ancient, splintered wood speaks to us, as if beckoning a reality
of days gone by.
Leaning itself to an understanding that life holds precious that better
part within us all,
Allowing our past sacrifice to remind us of the joy found living in the
present, with a lasting hope for future days.

*Inspired by of an old, broken-down barn I noticed while in a field photographing
wildflowers. It sat on a friend's farmland, and he explained that his grandfather
built the barn many years ago. My friend didn't have the heart to tear it down.
Good for him!*

The Living Path

Down a vintage road, bent and curved, as if its passage claimed age for a toll, the travels of certain souls continue to pay homage due.

Longing for refuge of better days and choices of youth made in haste, without thought of tomorrow, their hope lies fading.

Remembrance of sunlight, warm and inviting, haunt hidden dreams lost, as forlorn memories seldom allow for ease of seasons past.

Yet their nature pushes forward to perceivable understanding of discourse chosen and love left behind, though lonely and cold.

Time lived both abrupt and slow, now relinquished to the reminding reality of nearing end, for its price requires the commodity of youth.

So let the living path carry its sinuous length to term, and may their prognosis of justice delayed be filled with mercy and heaven's grace.

The Deep Places of My Heart

Somewhere hidden in the deep places of my heart lies a distant
memory of you.
Rough and jagged the edges scrape away treasures of once lived
dreams.
Melodies that long to remain sweet refrains of spring showers and
summer breezes,
Now haunt those songs of espoused love with bitter winds of change
and loss.

Where do we go to recapture those youthful impressions filled with
fervor?
How can we again visit a solitary shore that offers little more than the
sands of time washed away to the sea?
Gather quick and hold dear remnants of places and plans before they
vanish,
For future dreams of sworn adulation disappear as a star in the
morning sky.

Smiles and gentle tears mix together mildly when my dreams bring you
home,
Wishes of togetherness have long been replaced with numbing desires
of slumber.
We should have danced, when instead our actions lead us to nights of
betrayal,
We could have laughed, though chosen first where wasted words of
venom.

Still, lies a thought of color filled mountains high and beautiful to see,
Streams clear and cold, autumn days clinging to the hillside with my
hand in yours.
Beauty that is better felt than seen was captured in your gleaming eyes,
And today and together was the gift freely given to us both, now, once
again reminds me of you.

The Redeeming Strength of Love

On this dark dawning, let not the wounded weakness of calloused caring rise to meet the broken claim of dutiful remorse, bound by fear.

How can it so quickly be that our small asked offering of inner fortitude is now watched, as it crumbles and dissolves away in mere days of divisive doubt?

Are we not the sons and daughters of generations emergent of sacrificial greatness, of whom evil nations were altered for the betterment of mankind?

When the demands of our distorted return are met and children of God are forever lost, for then what will be the oblation of justice, as certainly we will be judged?

Surely the resolve of communal design and national character runs through deeper rivers than those, where swift yet shallow currents break.

There is no need of armed forces to protest against a foe of invisible disease, so do not let the hollowness of false bravado be our acceptance of choice.

For in its stead, project the proclaimed promises of celestial hope and purpose to show our unity of courage and shared suffering for its worthy end.

Then in its time, the commodity of truth and comforting light, will assert unified victory of joint resolve, in the redeeming strength of love in liberty's call.

For a concerned hope that our national character of resolve and love of our fellow man is stronger than it appears in these days of COVID-19.

If Not In Me

In the hard places of divisive chide and blame, where can the voice of love be found, if not in me?

Within segregated streets once envisioned a sheltered place, where can the eyes of love be seen, if not in me?

Because hateful hearts remain bitter and cold, where can the acceptance of love be felt, if not in me?

When vengeance is sought by the power of men, applauded with laud, where is the mercy of love shown, if not in me?

As acts of harmonic kindness are set aside for forces of self-righteous worth, where is the rescue of love formed, if not in me?

This is the declarative freedom of all who continue to ask only, where is the beginning touch of love raised, if not in me?

As the dismay of societal discourse continues to grow and expose our broken American hearts, the reality that I need to look inward first for answers resonates the loudest.

Praise

On this given day of life and breath, may our words of praise be heard at Heaven's gate, with thankfulness to sing.

Whether morning bright or clouds anguished above in gloom, allow the penned praise of humanity to claim their worth.

Let it be in us, as in our celestial home of glory, consumed with angelic choirs of celebrated praise, for Him on the Throne.

This is our heavenly required respite of repose to offer freely this grace, as was endowed in kind to us, the gift of praise.

Children of Israel, with begotten praise, laud the God of Exodus and freedom, as liberty exalts best in Kingdom's truth.

For joyous foundation of worth, both sublimely seen and heard, projects the love of saving grace through praise.

The Samaritan Way

Shelter us Lord beyond that which whispers low the fear of our own human frailty and weaknesses of the unknown.

Let us turn to Thee and again receive the reclamation of the promise by Your eternal grace that forever awaits both sufficient and strong.

During days of doubt, bring the vigor of life sustaining blood for us to proclaim the greatness of Your being to a nation in need of healing.

Lead us now from the temptation of slanting truth and placing blame on innocent souls of suffering, so to seek moments of vain reprieve.

Unite us Almighty God, that in our togetherness we display Your good and glorious compassion of the Samaritan's way.

For it is, that suffering and pain are engraved in humanity and thus becomes our Christian task to continue the praise of God and service to mankind.

Composed in concern and prayers for our nation and the world, as we all face the fears and frustration of an unknown and pandemic disease.

"The second is equally important: Love your neighbor as yourself. No other commandment is greater than these." Mark 12:31

"Then a despised Samaritan came along, and when he saw the man, he felt compassion for him . . . the Samaritan soothed his wounds with olive oil and wine and bandaged them . . . ." Luke 10:33-34

Upon the Sparrow

As this dark and fearful day marks the generational calling of our time, let us dwell now in Your spiritual grace of love.

Keep us from doubt and quick judgment of the unknown, as our shared purpose repeatedly clouds hearts with blame.

Seemingly with ease are forgotten the praises and joy of better light, in moments of temporal struggle and loss.

May it be both seen and felt that the promissory issues of hope are not abated over embattled life, looming with void.

Yet grant us seeds of faith beyond this day of earthly disregard and remember first Your eye upon the sparrow.

For not the destruction of a season will be our offering of trust, but instead acceptance that God is still on His heavenly throne.

From the scriptural promise and hymn, His Eye Is On the Sparrow.

Protection of Your Shadow

On this sun filled and present dawn, grant only, Lord, the protection of but Your shadow, as unknown fear surrounds me.

Give unto Your servant's hand the loving solitude of a peaceful valley walk in the morning mist of troubled times.

As nations tremble and projected proclamations of self-righteous worth continue, let us dwell only in the promise of Your celestial grace.

For our compliance of love and life eternal awaits not in the assurance of mankind, but that of cross borne and price paid submission.

May the Master of the sea once again lift us from the doubt of smashing waves against the tide of fear and human disease.

As He gently places us on the shore of faith and trust, accepting all that His heavenly mercy allows to endure, for yet this, too, shall pass.

Calvary's Cross of Love

May this morning of Hosannas be heard first in praise for the risen Lord, as our spiritual feet touch the sands of Jordan's shore.

Then no stone too vast or piercing sword sharp, will contain the glory of God from fulfillment of earthly cross and grave.

The cobblestone path leads not to death's door, but the awakening of life eternal through the power and promise of celestial grace.

Keep us Father from a dismal darkness, filled with void of life's giving breath, so we may proclaim this day for the living.

Remind us now of Your envisioned love, laced with mercy and simple kindness, to replace our own failed humanity.

For judgment of Heaven is Yours to hold, the price of sadden sin has since been laid and borne at Calvary's Cross of love.

The Good Fight

The colors of youth still paint my dawn with vivid flowers of love, as spring seeks its due and birds fill the skies with song.

Amid concerns only once imagined, life now calls for a voice of reason, longingly laced with mercy and heaven's touch.

Spirits desire to run with deep progeny throughout free land and feel warming sands, as they kiss the water's edge.

But as seasons turn, turn, turn* yet again, scripture reminds of purposeful time and place, requiring sacrifice today for praise of morning sun.

Can enduring strength of national character be the daunting challenge of defeat or the communal answering of worldly prayers?

Let this be the dawning of equality and truth suffered, yet risen above, by the good fight, persevered with gratitude and grace.

As we continue to battle and struggle nationally with pandemic disease and social discourse, and answer the question of what our American sacrifice will be.

Ecclesiastes 3:1-8
Pete Seeger 1959 and The Byrds 1965

For a Love She Never Knew

For a love she never knew, the poet's words fell silent and cold, sliding quietly into the dark night of misfortune.

For a love she never knew, roses stayed beautifully arrayed on the vine awaiting tomorrow for another admirers' touch.

For a love she never knew, his dreams remain dormant and still, untold, as visions of what might have been, while haunting the moonlight.

For a love she never knew, her greatest strengths and stronger passions of life were moving reminders of his weakness and doubt.

For a love she never knew, seasons of forfeited fervor grew into misplaced compassion, settling softly into a gentle sadness.

For a love she never knew, his dreams disappeared in a distant memory of beauty and truth, forlorn in a lost possibility of togetherness.

Love on the Fourth of July

Oh nations, of God's giving earth, listen to our song, as we proudly sing America's tune.
The power of its sweet refrain echoes across golden waves of wheat and field,
And rings the sound of Lady Liberty throughout the prodigious mountain tops of freedom's land.
For this country of immigrants once again looks past its sins of youth and proclaims justice for all.

This our creed, this our constitutional pursuit of human happiness, a claim not reserved for only wealth and privilege,
But for common and the masses, where our fore-fathers both sought and fought for better tomorrows, than this lone today.
Accept now the lost, the hurt, and down-trodden of life's luster, forlorn and forgotten, a generation surrendered for sons and daughters yet unborn.
This was their promise, their destiny of sacrifice, not to be ignored by years of intolerance and subjugation.

Live this day of gracious gifts, in our homeland that speaks for more than mere rights, civil and nation alike.
For scope and indulgence aligned, without empathy of brother unseen or race unknown, lies distant of victory's shore.
Shelter us each under the wings of heavenly spirit and watch the youth of eagles soar beyond imagination,
Experience then the magnitude of light, truth, hope, and enduring latitude of liberty, as love once again is found on the 4th of July.

Clay of Divine Love

Lord of Heaven, show Your allowance in all of its glory to find that lost part of me.
Accept my prayer of trust, with its special plea to be enough to become a part of You.
Push me in my belief to uncover that portion of doubt, hidden and dark,
Which requires a purer faith than what I now sadly possess.

Precious Son, lead me to my knees, bruised and weak from too much of my own doing,
Place me, Your creation, in the shadow of the Cross, beckoning its sorrow to become my joy.
Display Your wonder of daily life resembling Your holy acceptance,
With the potter's wheel, mold the existence of my heart with clay of divine love.

Entwine us Yahweh of the universe, to be in the precious here and now with You.
Command Your will to shower the blessings of favor and mercy upon mankind,
So we may combine Your strength to be that of our own, Your grace to touch a life given.
This is my prayer, which seeks both belief and faith, built upon the pillars of trusting You.

The Tolling Bell of Freedom

As the warm, setting sun gave its gentle way to the western shore, the tolling bell of freedom rang, with its last sad refrain.

Fields of golden life and mountain tops glazed in purple hue hold tight to their beauty in the morning mist, for first tears of wounded justice must flow.

Who today will stand on Memorial steps of sacrificed liberty and demand equality and truth of broken promises penned, once made to cover sins of disregard?

Who tomorrow will cross bridges of injustice to be met with daylight beatings and nighttime jailing of innocent people seeking only to breathe free?

The lost lunch counters of hate and disdain carried with them his blood, as he bravely led others onward to rise up against subjugated south-lands.

Humbled at self reflection and mild with mercy, he held a kindness of kinship for all shared suffering from inequality, as he remained embolden at Liberty's call.

Demand now, too, both youth and age, for voices heard and votes cast to honor his courageous continuance, so this righteous reformation moves onward.

For the day is now and the anthem heard, rings not uncertain for anyone other than the answering in twain, from the hearts of love in you and me.

Written in memoriam to civil rights leader, Congressman John Lewis. "Therefore, send not to know for whom the bell tolls, It tolls for thee."

~ John Donne

For the Fallen

As the morning dawns over majestic mountains and country sides laced with purple skies, our patriotic hearts cry out this day for the fallen.

In their ultimate sacrifice we both mourn and rejoice they would willingly bestow all, as weight of death's design lingers in memoriam.

Shall heavens shout out their calling in proclamation to generations yet unborn, and never taken for granted their dutiful legacy, now sealed in blood?

If indeed reverence in totality was for price paid, freely given, which has been sown as emancipated seed, on land, sea, and sky, then, too, our voices must sing hosanna in unison.

For the American love song, which lacks lyrics of liberty's demands, longing to sing, will never pay true homage to those deserving and honored few.

Island Beauty

Deep blue skies, deeper still the turquoise waters reflecting the gemstones of God's love.
Stormed tossed waves crashing the surf and sand, demanding human attention.
Nature's beauty offers its reward to only the quiet and attentive,
And so we listen to the silence of something greater than ourselves.

As golden sun warms the heart of poets and lovers alike,
Allow, oh Earth, the lunar tides to pull us all closer to thee.
Remind our nature that we are one and united from the stardust in our blood to the passions of our hearts.
Separate stance and indifference from lessons that lean to understanding.

Dare us each to view you from this perspective and deny your future existence.
Your majestic mountains that filter to the warmth of your winded waters,
Pull the masses to the white sanded shores of more than you and me.
Protecting you, caring for you, reveling in the awe of you will strengthen our humanity.

And in totality of this star filled sky, beaming light from worlds that no longer exist,
Let this night be one that shines more than emotions, more than ideas,
But that of determined commitment which extends beyond mere words of love.
For only through action will this island beauty remain our future to inherit.

First inspired by a trip to Hawaii, starting on the beach in a bungalow at Bellows AF Base and ending back home on a cold winter night in Tennessee. May humanity protect what God has given us dominion over . . . Mother Earth.

———————◆◆◆———————

Love's Sweet Falling

Who will touch the sky with love's sweet falling, as fear rises and lingers in the shadows of unknown tomorrows?

May this be the dawning of hope and promise, which leads to proclaimed unity of courage and yet professed devotion.

Search the gift of glorious light, collectively shining forth, garnished with grace and understanding of troubled times.

Let mercy abundant follow in the streams of desert sands to bring forth the goodness found in our earthly souls.

Lead us not from the shared sacrifice of today, but to embrace the solitude of strength found within committed hearts.

For only You exemplify truth of heavenly faith needed, compliant and resolute, to shower down celestial grace upon us all.

Granted Grace

The loss of beauty and love, entwined with precious time, leans itself to thoughts of you and seasons past.

Warming waters lightly kiss the sands, as dreams once again emerge of the soften touch of redden lips, as the sun slowly sets.

But sadden nights claim their dutiful price, for the web and flow of fervid tides are a never ceasing reminder of deceitful debt.

Aged questions of worthy cost are better inked than felt, as hearts of passion easily break again and so again.

Still stars of far away skies glimmer with both hopes and smiles that horizons await new dawns, laced with risen love.

Years of exclusion and deserved pain have yet to pay the price of hurt caused, because granted grace was taken, but for granted denied.

Sweet Prince

In a haze of mixed color and emotion, his words spoke to our hearts,
as his music moved our bodies forward.
Caring little for the common, his resolve brought demands of lyrical
revolution and joyful noise to our ears.
Societal mirrors were his focus, yet his speech contained no hate,
and lovers everywhere now know why doves cry.
His genius lay calm in his mind, but screamed to the hillside
with the passions of youth and desire.

He portrayed the unspoken with a sensitive smile and tore away our
humanity, with both piercing and sympathetic verse.
Rainbows were his to paint, with lines that were better felt than
understood, as impulses of rhythm coursed through our veins down to
our souls.
Where did he go, and how often was he left to doubt, when the
daylight hushed his singing and the dancing faded from his council?
Our hearts protest his leaving, and our inner song seems dark and
distant, as we chant in unison of Purple Rain and Red Corvettes.

Why is it that the minstrel's tune of some touch our inner youth, in
ways that mere flowers in a fence pay homage due and prayers prayed?
Glory and praise given to that better part of us, as seen and felt in him
displayed in near perfect rhythm and blues.
Brought to you and me in measure with time, notes in tune with the
beat of our hearts and minds in tune with the reverence of our storied
lives.
This is what he did for me; he did for us all, as we shared vicariously
with his living now we must do with the reality of sadness in his
passing.

*For the love of music and song and its societal importance and in memoriam of
Prince. "Good night sweet prince, may angels of mercy take thee to thy rest."*
                                                          ~ Shakespeare's Hamlet

The Old Timer

I watched him, as he watched the game being played before us,
And as I imagined what it was once like for him to play,
His memory soared and then settled in an old and familiar place.
Granting him both the solace and freedom of younger days relived.

His feet casually, naturally spiked at the earth beneath him,
As it had so many times before, as it would again today.
A smile crossed his rugged face and there he was now, as even then,
The warmth of the spring sun could bring back no other thought than
the cry of, Play ball!

He could not escape the distant memories of his youth,
Nor could you take them from him for all the riches of today.
From the smell of fresh cut grass to the mix of sand and dirt,
It ran as deep through his blood, as it once did ground into his
uniform.

Caring only for the game and to play, he felt the slight breeze blow,
And fond, sweet memories from his boyhood past raced by,
As he now ached to wrap his strong fingers around fresh pine,
Swinging with new found purpose and timed to perfection.

To feel the power and hear again the crack of the bat
Was but his only desire, though on this noon his contentment
Will find its resting place deep within a pleasant memory,
Never to be erased, forgotten, or replaced.

For the Old Timer today was once again alive,
And he played not within his mind or body,
But throughout his heart, and the thrill of this game
Was never so sweet, nor everlasting.

Originally written while photographing a baseball tournament at Seven Oaks Park, home of the Twitty City Baseball Club in Nashville, TN. While viewing an Old Timer (Mr. Joe May) watching the game from behind the fence at home plate. Then, after his passing, dedicating this poem to Mr. May and presenting it to Mr. Jack Lavender, one of the founding members of The Old Timers Baseball Association, Nashville, TN chapter. To my knowledge Jack kept a copy of the original poem in his office until his passing.

One of my favorite memories (and there were many) of Mr. Lavender was when he told me that if I really wanted to increase my knowledge of baseball, "Just come to my office any morning, sit over there in that corner, and keep your damn mouth shut . . . you might just learn something." He was rough around the edges, a fountain of knowledge of this great game, and a generous, caring man. Plus, he was right! He did more for amateur baseball in Middle Tennessee than any other player or coach that I know. When I founded, owned, and operated a small non-profit corporation, Youth, Education, and Sports, Inc., we named our baseball scholarship fund after Mr. Lavender. It was my honor to help send a few young players to college to play baseball in Jack's name.

For the Magnitude of Grace

What opens the heart of our humanity to the magnitude of grace divine, with thankfulness abound, as false power professes hateful demise?

It is for this day and His majesty of life that we choose a brighter dawn, and a road less traveled,* to accept mercy offered and love given anew.

May our frail and humble benediction be worthy of heavenly light to restore a portion of hope for a lost and wayward soul, more deserving than our own.

The abuse of mere personal choice lay waste to redemptive glory, consumed justice with seven times seventy long passed and sadly displaced.

For the desire of innocence lies in generational longing for the refuge of younger days and precious time, once forgotten but remembered today.

May this prayer of Thanksgiving be brought from a protracted proclamation to a grander pursuit of purposeful love, to be both shared and sheltered.

For no other moment than now matters or carries the weight of aspirational design, as our knees bend and our hearts open for all to sublimely receive.

Robert Frost

My Remembrance of You

Ocean waves, rolling and gemstone blue, like the eyes of an island maiden,
Warm waters, and warmer still, only heighten the laden touch of your browning skin.
Those bold thoughts hold me close in past memories of both yesterday and today,
Where sands consumed the evening tide, as my hand trembled reaching for you in the morning sun.

We were lost together in that here and now, needing little more than a lover's sweet caress.
As a star filled night, kissed by the moonlight, spoke softly to the ocean breeze, come closer.
The sea that whispered your name now calls for fond recollections of us.
And we were one with the passions of youth, as well as the beat of our hearts.

Those were the days and nights of laughter with added tears of joy,
Tropical gardens surrounded laced pools of colors deep, as we gazed into each other's eyes.
The tenderness shared could not be captured by espoused words of love,
So our time was together for moments of dreams, now forgotten and lost.

May was the month of our making, spring was the season of our passion.
Happiness existed because of you, as your smile would light the night.
This is my choice of both worlds once living, given life again anew.
For contentment has its place, but not in the shadow of my remembrance of you.

Away in Time

Silent and fading the once held dream of a future filled with togetherness and you, finds itself in a dark and dusty corner of my soul.

Smiles and tears entwine leaving my heart to ache and sing out for that part of you, of us, that brought joy to the mundane and happiness to life.

To touch your hand stirred desire, and control of emotions were lost in our closeness, as stars filled the night with our love.

How can the light of the day bring its warmth without soaring thoughts of your smile, captured within a vision of eternal bliss?

Those hours passing when laughter cushioned our hearts and dance our steps, while loneliness was only a concept left to the forgotten past.

For the telling of every kiss was seen in the deepening color of your eyes, as the breaking of every heart drifts away in time.

Love Yet Remains

In this solace and quiet, there is no peace to find.
Darkness that fills the night, fills also our hearts,
As children cry, as mothers weep.
Words no longer suffice, and actions are long in coming,
Bring on the new day and let its sun sing a sweeter refrain.

The ocean that separates the pain deepens, too, the hurt,
And there is no comfort to give when none can be explained.
The loss is greater than imagination of strength,
For some pain freedom cannot ease.
Tears must flow, hearts must break, as time ceases to exist.

Winds that blew the Caribbean nights cool are stagnant now,
And the stench of death rises, as hope fades distant and still.
Where are the strong when the weak need us most?
What will we reply when their tears ask us but why?
For fears of humanity often outweigh intentions of good.

Oh, Land of Liberty stop not at nature's cruel calling;
Send forth your dominion of gifts, demand from all their best.
Now is the time given, with only a small sacrifice to make.
Let us choose this day for whom by faith we will serve.
Showing to all within our reach that love yet remains.

Dedicated to Haiti, Puerto Rico, the Dominican Republic, their citizens, and their devastated homelands in the aftermath of Hurricane Maria in 2017.

Sing For the Children

Sing for the children with a voice of strength and praise,
Proclaiming hope for tomorrow and gladness of this precious now.
Validate their feelings with a ballad of justice and peace,
Show them caring with melody and tune of glory and grace.

Sing for the children and accept them as one into this world,
Allowing your words to caress gently with mercy and love.
Make lyrics worthy of heavenly hosannas blessed by human devotion,
And assure them of songs to sing that reveal the heart of their youth.

Sing for the children and be careful of the example to set,
Knowing tender souls are within our grasp of love, compassion or
scorn.
Share your talent of harp and song with a smile of contentment,
For within a face of sweet refrain they will envision a place of joy.

Sing for the children and set a lifetime path of melodic prose,
Challenging imaginations and ensuring pleasant memories to come.
Give tenderness and beauty of talent and gift, as given to you.
As you share of yourself to help fulfill the wonderment of life.

*Inspired (and written in part) by the Patty Griffin song, Be Careful, as covered by
Amy at Hope Park Church (now Spero Dei) one Sunday morning past. But
mostly this poem was written because of Amy's beautiful voice and heartfelt
testimony, as she both broke and mended my heart in the same moment by sharing
her talent of song.*

It Is Not Only

For it is not only the soft and golden sunset that loans its beauty to the seaward sky that makes the poet bring pen to hand and compose sonnets of love.

It is not only the dew on the rose or her sweet and gentle scent, which caresses our heart and turns our thoughts to dream of loves long ago.

It is not only the cool mountain morning, crisp with nature's sole refrain, that demands our prayers of praise for things we cannot comprehend.

But, too, is the desire that lies deep within, and calls our name wildly, saying, "Share these wonders graciously given," for us to know truth and value of what beauty life holds.

Love's Lost Rhyme

With skeptic vision of a brief look in time,
Brought memory to bare love's lost and fleeting rhyme.
It lingers sweetly in silence but a moment long,
As spring proclaims in refrain a robin's soft song.

No discourse can weigh and later view,
To bring forth romance and justice due.
For cost required was paid with sadden tears,
As each day passes through lonely years.

But be not dismayed or hope despair,
Love still grows and wraps with care.
The drawing heart will picture most,
The stars that fall with heavenly hosts.

So shout the glory beyond discovery found,
To wondrous nature of grace abound.
For it must be now, as tomorrow and then,
Touched ever so gentle by God's eternal hand.

Let

Let the morning heart sing praises of Hosanna most high, so the breath of life may be given for the living to live.

Let the spoken word that first brought light, speak again with venerated grace to be shared, never rationed for self-worth.

Let the voices of His people intone truth and trust, accepting mercy above what is deserved, adulation beyond us.

Let the glory of God on the Throne be felt, both seen and alive, for those that hope has become lost and hidden as dust.

Let the fullness of His heavenly spirit inspire us to be more than our humanity allows, as acceptance imparts faith.

Let the sacrifice of our Lord and Savior remain the forwarding thrust of our proclaimed beliefs to love one another.

The Family Ties

Faded away and placed in a corner closet lies a photograph that once depicted a vision of love and family.

Reserved for no one and no one longer sees the reality of similar face and smile, once treasured, now forgotten.

The splintered wood frame holds tighter to the memory of vision than does the blood in our connected veins, and life flows onward.

There is no fault in the reality of passing time, as the importance of linage exists less and less, with a world that spins in the ever presence of today.

Yet a pleasant thought of heritage should hold its place within us all, for they lived that we should have life and yesterday paves the road traveled today.

The battle of youth versus age lingers with each generation and must find its own resolve to determine its valued worth,

For if our past does not receive its just regard, then, no doubt, the repetition of its failure will exist far into future lives and worlds.

Cling to that which justifies its relevant demand, and push onward with a connected memory of sacrificial souls that gave allowance to our progression.

And if in transient relation there comes a peace and permanence to those who came before, then relish in its existence and smile.

For this is all they wish, an acknowledgment from a future child, an endowment of their being, so a worthiness surpasses time and place.

A voice to the stars that their living was not in vain, their choices not in void by the simple reluctance of time itself,

So in the finality of this envisioned page, discolored and browning edges all, will proclaim its hope, faith, and embrace for whomever takes a moment to see and feel the family ties.

Inspired by an old family photograph of my Uncle M.C. Headrick and his wife, Edna Earl (ironically also my mother's name, his sister's) found by my daughter on a social media page that I didn't even know existed. It moved me to think of all the wonderful family stories of my mother and her 11 siblings and their profound influence on the lives of my sisters, myself and our children. In particular, I remember how he once performed a small, but significant, act of love for me, when I was working for him in one of his grocery stores, at the age of 19. It embedded such a sweet memory of him with me that I will cherish it and him, as I have, for the rest of my life!

A Summer Storm

It rained today, surprisingly and as it should have.
The appropriateness of nature lending itself to a melancholy mood,
And sought out by hearts broken and questions asked, with answers
hurtful and known.

The thunder booming, as if to say, Your sadness and lost is shared by
the wind.
As a summer storm tosses the lover's heart without regard of feeling,
seeking to place it deep, dark beyond the bonds of repair.

The sun dared to shine, as I dared not to think of you, both useless and
discarded efforts of sad remorse.
Brought against such natural forces of clash and rain, of love and
passion.

Now, as sounds of thunder die away into the heat of this night,
And bolts of light, once reserved for descriptions of our love, fade
distant and quiet across the evening sky.

My heart cries out in wonder, searching for more than these mere
words of comfort can bring.
Brought forth from somewhere lost and hidden, only to hear in fevered
return the echo of your name.

Your Magical Dance

Oh dance your magical dance and call on the dawn to prepare life, yet again, for a radiant beginning of starlight.

Offer no haste of reservation or delinquency of time, as the season of now beckons your youthful response.

Consume the day and digest it for nourishing strength to conquer over the disease of darkness and stain.

Move forward with the expedient desire to choose life on the terms of its origin, filled with passion and glee.

Make your difference of worth be that which is tipped with tolerant compassion and not gathered gold of greed.

For you were made of love and not a legacy of forgotten dust, which collectively requires the union of heavenly design.

A Turn of Seasons

There are often deep and dark moments, somewhere lost in the night, easier felt than seen.
Already missing what is yet to take place, I reach inside of me for what you have touched and again given life anew.

Longing for both the pain and pleasure to linger, where yesterday we lay close and together.
Shinning forth from the light of the night, finding more than mere reflection of distant rays upon the autumn moon.

Now that we are reminded that life is only made great by living and only challenged by change,
Take with you the better part of me, these words, hidden forever within your heart.

Perhaps some day hence, holding them close and dear, they will warm a cold and lonely twilight passing.
For as seasons present surely turn to seasons past and hearts to lover's hearts,

May you always wish to turn back to me and smile with a special thought of love.
Not only for what was felt or spoken, but for what dreams might have been lived, if only fate and time were kinder to us both.

Beyond the Window

Can you look beyond the window, through the heart's storm and past the night?
Can you answer love's sweet calling hastened onward, brighter than mere candlelight?
Is there waiting, silent and patient, someone, somewhere not far from this day,
To share in life's giving, complete with joy, willful to allow a better way?

Can you look beyond the window, to where the sea runs calm and deep?
Can you answer love's sweet calling, words to whisper, and share in a lover's restful sleep?
Decisions made from past impressions leave to doubt young hearts with dreams.
Go to view thy own chosen treasures enhanced by more than often seems.

Can you look beyond the window to the place I see where beauty lies?
Can you answer love's sweet calling the way it sings from within your eyes?
The touch will take you far away to places beside me you never knew,
But you must seek and desire its wishes and allow it to be a part of you.
Can you look beyond the window?

Love is . . .

Love is multifaceted and consists of varying degrees and levels of empathy and heart, while hate exists as the broken part of our humanity, where evil originates.

Love is conversant of thought and is often difficult, requiring us to engage with mercy, kindness, and forgiveness. It is consumptive of animus and misery, as well as nurturing of our better angels.

Love is universal and unites us both in joy and pain, victory and defeat, the spring and fall of our lives, as we celebrate living and morn death.

Love is strengthening and gives hope and purpose to our earthly existence. It is festive reception when there should be none. It is understanding where none is deserved.

Love is redemptive and often bridges personal reformation, as it restores unfulfilled dreams and releases its unknown power and mystery.

Love is a shared courtship of dreams, desires, and promises of the heart. It exists to be enjoyed, yet seldom is multiplicative without selfless sacrifice.

Love is boundless by time or space and carries with it the past, present, and future of unconditional resolve.

Love is truth and light, for it requires trust and spiritual want to mask and dissolve away our fallible frailties.

Love is heavenly designed to be issued and communal, yet seeks nothing in return, as its magnitude and reversion is in direct equity to its beginning legacy.

Love is the accumulate answer to every unknown question that causes grief, sorrow, compassion, happiness, and acceptance.

Love is . . . love.

ACKNOWLEDGMENTS

I sincerely wish to acknowledge the support and love of my two children, Candice and Donovan, my precious granddaughter Stella Rose, and all of my family and friends who, without their lifetime of caring, support, and concern, my poems would not reflect the true feelings found written in these words of love.

ABOUT THE AUTHOR

I. Stevens is the chosen pseudonym for writer Steve Reed, a retired Language Arts teacher, academic advisor, photographer, and business owner. He currently resides in a rural community outside of Nashville, Tennessee and continues to write poetry, short stories, and essays during his retirement years. His first book of poems, entitled *My 40 Days*, inspired by his personal struggle with cancer, was published in 2020. He is also the author of *The Diverged Road* and the forthcoming, *My American Christmas*.

PERSONAL REFLECTIONS